In the Name of Allah.

To all who can appreciate the womb; the humble beginning shared by all of mankind.
Warm and rent-free.

www.prolancewriting.com
California, USA
©2017 Hira Khan
Illustrations ©2017 Jenny Renish

All rights reserved. No part of the publication may be reproduced in any form without prior permission from the publisher.

ISBN :978-0-615-85287-4
Edited by Shoilee Khan

A Gift from Jannah

Written by Hira Khan
Illustrated by Jenny Reynish

*With Love,
♡ hira
2017*

PROLANCE

Long ago, high up in a cloud, I walked with an Angel in Jannah. Every day, as the sun rose and turned the clouds pink and then golden, I asked my Angel, "Is it time yet?".

Down below, on the green, green earth, I knew my parents were waiting. Allah picked them just for me.

He placed a special love between their hearts and now they wanted it to grow. So every day, as the sky glowed orange and red from the disappearing rays of the sun, my parents prayed to Allah.

They asked Him to bless them with a child. *"O Allah, grant me offspring from the righteous,"* they whispered.

Their prayers floated up from the green, green earth, through the misty clouds, all the way to Allah.

There was some delightful chatter and anticipation in Jannah. All the heavenly angels excitedly spread the word to one another about the prayer that arrived.

Allah told the Angels that it was time for me to slip into my mom's womb. It was a long journey and I fell fast asleep.

When I woke up, I found myself in a warm, soft and quiet room with lots of space. Floating inside, I could hear the *thunka, thump thump, thunka thump, thump* of my mom's heart.

I could hear voices, too. The soft, sweet voice was my mom's. The strong, reassuring voice was my dad's.

What did they look like? When would I meet them? I would have to wait. I would have to grow.

So, I grew and grew and grew.

Mom's tummy grew and grew and I grew too! Mom walked with a funny waddle. Dad's hugs warmed mom's tummy and his voice reciting the Quran would ripple through the womb and surround me.

Some nights, my mom could not stay still. She would toss and turn the whole night. She whispered prayers and I knew her words were spinning through the starry sky to Allah.

"The moon is shining bright, little one. For you my child, I have prayed," she whispered.

I slept deep during the day, but mom patted her tummy and talked to me about all the magical treasures I would soon see.

"Here is a bear with brown sugar fur. Here is a soft, knitted blanket to keep you warm. Here are white satin booties for your tiny, tiny toes." Dad and mom were counting down the days until we met. "Just two more weeks," I heard dad say. Soon, I would leave mom's womb.

It was my home. It was safe and warm and I could hear the *thunka, thump thump* of her heart. Would I hear her heart when I left?

"Just one more week!" I heard dad laugh, his arms warm around mom's tummy. I listened to the *thunka, thump thump, thunka thump thump* of mom's heart.

I didn't want to leave. I wanted to stay warm and safe forever.

"Come out, little one!" I heard dad say, his voice worried. "You're a little late. You must be comfy in there."

I slept and slept, listening to the *thunka thump thump* of mom's heart. One evening, when mom was resting, I heard her voice clear and strong. *"O Allah, please give me a child with good manners. O Allah, please give me a child that is strong, healthy, and has eyes that shine with Your light at everything You created."*

Then, mom whispered softly to me. "Little one, the moon is shining bright again. It's shining for me and for you. Come see what Allah has created for you. Come see the moon and the stars, and the green, green earth. I will hold you in my arms, warm and snug against my chest. My heart will beat for me and for you."

It was quiet. I knew mom's prayer had swirled through the stars, around the moon, and up to Allah. I knew because I felt my warm, safe room move around me. I felt the firm walls of mom's womb pulse against my body.

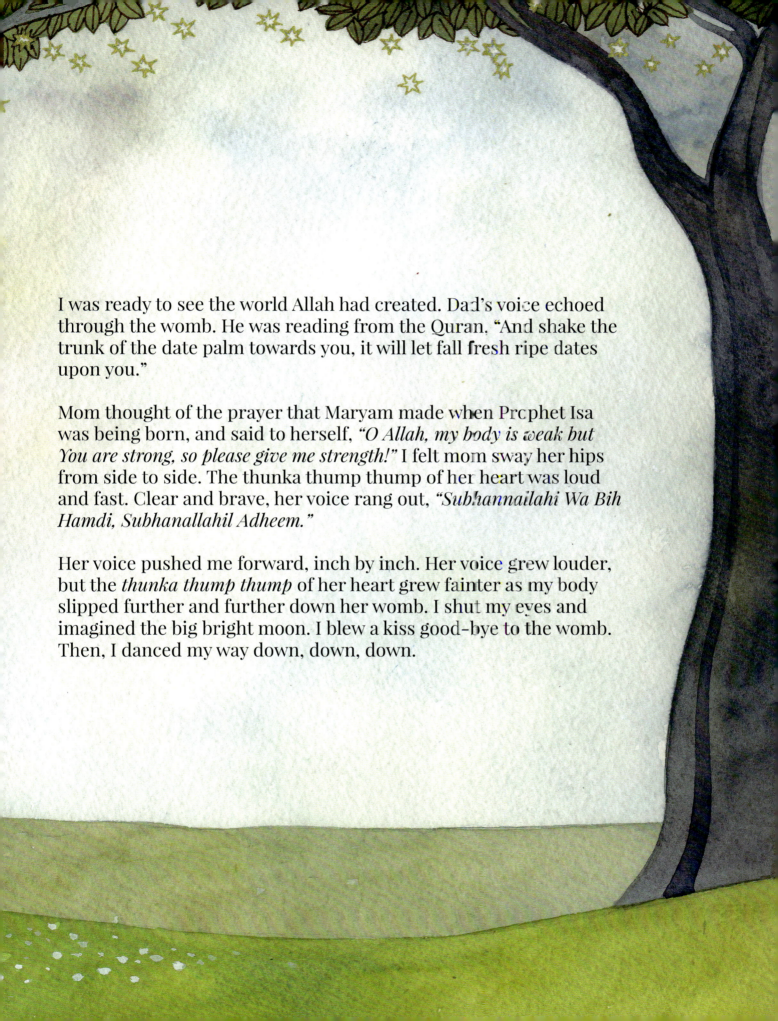

I was ready to see the world Allah had created. Dad's voice echoed through the womb. He was reading from the Quran. *"And shake the trunk of the date palm towards you, it will let fall fresh ripe dates upon you."*

Mom thought of the prayer that Maryam made when Prophet Isa was being born, and said to herself, *"O Allah, my body is weak but You are strong, so please give me strength!"* I felt mom sway her hips from side to side. The thunka thump thump of her heart was loud and fast. Clear and brave, her voice rang out, *"Subhannailahi Wa Bih Hamdi, Subhanallahil Adheem."*

Her voice pushed me forward, inch by inch. Her voice grew louder, but the *thunka thump thump* of her heart grew fainter as my body slipped further and further down her womb. I shut my eyes and imagined the big bright moon. I blew a kiss good-bye to the womb. Then, I danced my way down, down, down.

The cold air of the earth prickled my skin.

I was out!

I heard a familiar sound. A sound from Jannah. It was the Adhaan and it was dad whose voice I heard, hot and clear in my ear.

Then he smeared something sweet and thick over my lips and gums. Yummy! "This is tahneek, my baby," dad smiled. "Your first taste of the world is sweet with these honeyed dates."

"My little one," I heard a voice whisper. My mom.

My cheek pressed against her chest, her strong arms around me, I felt my eyes slowly close.

There, soft but strong, I heard it – the *thunka thump thump* of her heart. I opened my eyes.

Thank you, Allah.

Mom looked at me with wide eyes. Dad looked at mom with love. They snuggled me close.

"Our gift from Jannah has arrived!"

Glossary

Adhaan:	Call to Prayer
Allah:	God
Jannah:	Heaven
Tahneek:	The Prophetic practice that takes place after birth. The newborn is given a taste of dates, rubbed against the gums.
Dhikr Prayer:	Subhanallahi Wa Bih Hamdi, (Glory be to Allah, and His is the Praise) Subhanallahil Adhim (the Greatest is free from imperfection)
Surah Maryam:	19th chapter of the Quran, named after Mary, Mother of Jesus
Quran:	Sacred book of Islam

The Author

Hira Khan is the creator and founder of BirthKeeper, providing Doula Services in the Toronto area and Prenatal Education to the global Muslim community since 2009.

As a Canadian trained Labor Doula, Hira believes that every woman is the hero of her own birth story. Hira has been mentored by several influential teachers of birth. Hira has traveled and studied at birthing centers around the world. Hira's background in alternative medicine allow her to bring a holistic and natural approach to her practice.

In her spare time, she works to build bridges through social advocacy, encourages interfaith projects and dialogue within her community. Hira is an old soul at heart and enjoys history, reading and yoga. Hira resides in Milton, Ontario with her two sweet souled boys and loving husband.

Visit **www.birthkeeper.ca** for resources and downloads.

The Illustrator

Jenny Reynish lives and works near Colchester in Essex, UK. She works as a freelance illustrator, having produced illustrations for various publishers of books and magazines in the UK and USA, as well as card designs. Much of the inspiration for her work is drawn from things seen and experienced while traveling; as well as from the imagination.

She enjoys incorporating elements of ethnic and folk art, and details inspired by those in Persian carpets and woodcarvings, in addition to imagery from nature, cities and buildings. Fish, birds, elephants and angels appear as recurring motifs. She uses a variety of media, including oil, watercolour, egg tempera and acrylic.

Visit **www.magiccarpetpics.co.uk** to view Jenny's portfolio.

Information technology

Pennie Stoyles, Peter Pentland, and David Demant

This edition first published in 2004 in the United States of America by
Smart Apple Media.

All rights reserved. No part of this book may be reproduced in any form or by any means without written permission from the publisher.

Smart Apple Media
1980 Lookout Drive
North Mankato
Minnesota 56003

Library of Congress Cataloging-in-Publication Data

Stoyles, Pennie.
  Information technology / Pennie Stoyles, Peter Pentland, and David Demant.
    p. cm. — (Science issues)
  Summary: Discusses two sides of issues related to information technology—how carefully the Internet should be controlled, whether information on the Internet should be subject to copyright laws, and how much information should remain in electronic storage indefinitely.
  ISBN 1-58340-329-9
  1. Information technology—Juvenile literature. [1. Information technology. 2. Internet.] I. Pentland, Peter. II. Demant, David. III. Title.
  T58.5.S75 2003
  303.48'33—dc21   2002044635

First Edition
9 8 7 6 5 4 3 2 1

First published in 2003 by
MACMILLAN EDUCATION AUSTRALIA PTY LTD
627 Chapel Street, South Yarra, Australia 3141

Associated companies and representatives throughout the world.

Copyright © Pennie Stoyles, Peter Pentland, and David Demant 2003

Edited by Sally Woollett
Text and cover design by Polar Design Pty Ltd
Illustrations by Alan Laver, Shelly Communications
Photo research by Jes Senbergs

Printed in Thailand

Acknowledgements
The author and the publisher are grateful to the following for permission to reproduce copyright material:

Cover photograph: computer chips, courtesy of Photolibrary.com

Australian Picture Library/Corbis, p. 24; brand X pictures, p. 27; Coo-ee Picture Library, pp. 5, 12, 13, 20, 25; Daimler Chrysler AG, p. 7; Getty Images, pp. 4, 9, 10, 11, 18; The Kobal Collection, p. 19; Dale Mann/Retrospect, p. 17; screen shots reprinted by permission from Microsoft Corporation Plus MS trademark, pp. 15 (bottom), 29; MIDS Matrix Maps at www.mids.org, p. 23; Photolibrary.com, pp. 6, 15 (top), 22, 26, 30; Redferns Music Picture Library, p. 21; Stock Photos, p. 28; Symantec, reproduced with permission, p. 14.

While every care has been taken to trace and acknowledge copyright, the publisher tenders their apologies for any accidental infringement where copyright has proved untraceable. Where the attempt has been unsuccessful, the publisher welcomes information that would redress the situation.

Contents

Information technology	4
Information technology is a science issue	5
Understanding information technology	6
ISSUE 1 Internet safety	10
The Internet safety debate	17
ISSUE 2 Information ownership	18
The Information ownership debate	23
ISSUE 3 Electronic storage of information	24
The electronic storage debate	29
Summary	30
Glossary	31
Index	32

Glossary words
When a word is printed in **bold** you can look up its meaning in the Glossary on page 31.

 Look out for these questions.
Try to think about them while you read each issue in this book.

Information technology

Three children and their father are waiting anxiously for their mother in an international airport departure lounge.

Their mother sends a text message to her husband on his mobile phone that her car has developed a serious fault. The car's computer detected the fault before it became too serious and advised her to stop. She uses her mobile phone again to call a tow company and a taxi.

While waiting at the airport, the father **downloads** an electronic book from the **Internet** into his laptop and reads it to his children. He keys in his credit card number to pay for the book.

At last the mother arrives at the departure lounge. The whole family passes through the security area. The information from their passports is recorded on computer. This computer can contact similar computers all over the world and tell them that the family has just passed through security.

All the information mentioned in this example is stored in computers.

Information technology is the name given to all the ways that computers can be used to process information. Computers can control the equipment we use and provide us with helpful information. They are very powerful tools and manufacturers are continually improving them.

Information technologists design computers and **computer programs**. They:
- find ways for us to communicate quickly and easily around the world using the Internet
- help to design programs that will stop people from stealing information
- design new ways to store information electronically.

Computers are designed to be used for many different functions.

Information technology is a science issue

What if computer information is misused?

Some people think computers and all the information that is processed by them can take away people's privacy. They worry that books or music can be illegally copied. Other people think that computers make life easier. There are also people who have not yet made up their minds. This makes information technology a science issue.

Different points of view

Sometimes you have to decide what you think about something. Before you decide whether something is good or bad, or right or wrong, you usually try to find out about the subject and listen to what other people think. There may be two opposite points of view. Different people or groups may have several different views. This is what makes something an issue.

Can you trust everything you read and hear? It is a good idea to look carefully at the people who are arguing about an issue. Do they know all of the facts? Are they only giving one side of the issue because they have something to gain? You should not simply accept what people say. Think about what they say and why they say it.

Think about the source of your information before you accept it.

THIS BOOK will help you understand more about some information technology issues. It tries to be balanced. Two sides of each issue are presented to help you to decide what *you* think.

You will:

- find out more about how computers process information
- decide if computers and the Internet affect our privacy
- find out how computers affect people's rights to what they create
- examine the good and bad points of storing computer information.

Understanding information technology

Computers can be used to write stories, draw pictures, create music, play games, send **e-mail**, and surf the **Web**.

How a computer works

When you press a key on the keyboard, an electric signal goes to the computer. The computer stores the signal in its **memory**. This is because the computer does lots of things while you are typing. It checks spelling, automatically saves your work, keeps itself running, and much more.

When the computer is ready, it processes the electric signal. The **processor** inside the computer changes the signal and sends it to the screen. The letter, number, or symbol on the key you pressed is now on the computer screen.

This sounds as if it takes a lot of time. But computers are very fast. You might take about half a second before you press the next key. Computers are able to do a thousand or more things in half a second!

We call the keyboard an **input device** because it puts information into the computer. A mouse and a camera are other input devices. The screen is an **output device** because it puts out what we want from the computer. A printer and speakers are other output devices. A computer takes inputs and produces the outputs we want.

Computers use devices such as microchips, hard drives, and disks to store information. These devices can also be used to input and output information to and from a computer.

Quick byte

The first computers filled whole rooms and weighed more than 1.1 tons (1 t). They were much slower than computers are today.

A computer can have many input and output devices connected to it.

Computers and machines

A computer is different from any other machine because computers are used to process information inside other machines.

A computer can be used in an automatic grass mower for a football field. A grass-mowing computer can use cameras to see when it gets to the edge of the grass and to go around goalposts. It also measures the length of the grass. The computer uses these inputs to change its direction or the height of the cutters—its outputs.

A computer can be used in a rocket. It measures the height above the ground, wind direction, and distance from the target. The computer uses these inputs to make the rocket travel to its target—the output that is required.

It does not matter to a computer what its inputs are. As long as the inputs can be changed into electrical signals, then it will process them to do the outputs required.

∧∧ This car is driven by a computer. The human "driver" uses a joystick to give the computer instructions.

Computers are also used in mobile phones, refrigerators, microwaves, medical equipment, car navigation systems, compact disc (CD) players, digital cameras, and tractors.

Computer programs

A program is a list of instructions that runs the computer. A computer program is like a translator from one language to another. It changes inputs into electrical symbols that the computer is designed to understand.

>>
One day many houses will be run by computers!

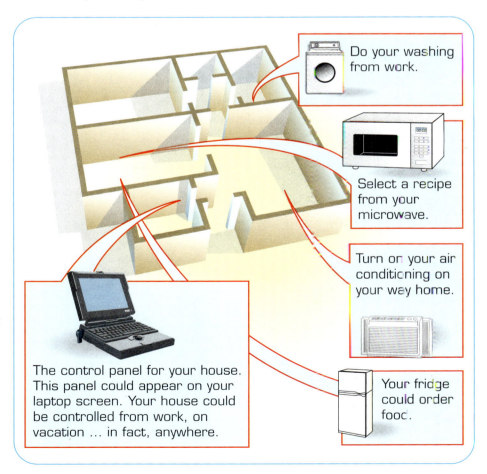

Do your washing from work.

Select a recipe from your microwave.

Turn on your air conditioning on your way home.

Your fridge could order food.

The control panel for your house. This panel could appear on your laptop screen. Your house could be controlled from work, on vacation … in fact, anywhere.

7

Computer language

A computer operates millions of very small electric switches. Each switch can be either on or off. Computer designers use 0 (zero) to show when the switch is off and 1 (one) when it is on. The code that uses only 0s and 1s is called binary code.

The statement "Hello 123." written in binary code looks like this:

> 01001000011001010110110001101100011011110110000001100010011001000110011001101101

When the stream of 0s and 1s is broken up, you can see that even the space between words and the full stop are in binary code.

H	e	l	l	o	word space	1	2	3	full stop
01001000	01100101	01101100	01101100	01101111	01100000	00110001	00110010	00110011	00101101

A table to convert to and from binary code

Step 1: write the row code.

Step 2: write the column code.

	0010	0011	0100	0101	0110	0111
0000		0		P	word space	p
0001	!	1	A	Q	a	q
0010	"	2	B	R	b	r
0011		3	C	S	c	s
0100		4	D	T	d	t
0101		5	E	U	e	u
0110		6	F	V	f	v
0111		7	G	W	g	w
1000		8	H	X	h	x
1001		9	I	Y	i	y
1010			J	Z	j	z
1011			K		k	
1100	comma		L		l	
1101	full stop		M		m	
1110			N		n	
1111			?	O		o

The binary code for A is 01000001

You can see from the table that each keyboard symbol has a code that is a combination of eight switches. Just imagine how many switches would be needed to store all the words and pictures in this book in the memory of a computer! Switches in computers are tiny. Millions of them fit into your computer.

The Internet

The Internet contains millions of computers connected in **networks** across the world. Your school network might be connected to all the other school networks in your area. The area network might be connected to a larger network. The Internet is a vast network of millions of networks.

Because all the computers are connected, you can use the Internet to send an e-mail, search for information, play games, make an airline booking, buy a book, or "talk" with a group of people anywhere in the world.

When you use the Internet, your computer may send a message to another computer called a **server**. Servers can store **Web sites**, update ticket information, and organize on-line conversations and games. Messages can also be sent to other computers directly, without using a server.

When your message travels via the Internet, special computers direct the messages to their destinations. These computers are called **network computers**. They are like air traffic controllers at airports.

Browsers

There are many different programs on a computer. Each has a different job to do. When people use the Internet to look for information, they may use a program called a **browser**. This searches through millions of **Web pages** stored on different servers. Other programs are used for e-mail, booking tickets, and so on.

Quick byte
The first message was sent on the Internet in October 1971.

^ All over the world, there are computers in offices, factories, schools, and homes—millions and millions of them.

ISSUE 1 Internet safety

Uninvited visitors

Imagine that you have bought a new computer. You send e-mails to friends and you search the Internet for music.

One day you are visiting a Web site. No matter how many times you click on the CLOSE button, it does not go away. It keeps on popping up. The people who run the Web site have changed the CLOSE button so it opens another Web page! You switch your computer off in frustration.

The next day, you switch on your computer and you have some e-mails. Some are from friends and others from people you do not know. One of these e-mails says, "Hello, there is a lovely present for you in this e-mail." It has an attachment, which you double-click to open. Nothing seems to happen. So you send another e-mail to some friends and switch off.

The next day, when you switch on your computer, you find that the text on your screen is jumbled up. A friend phones you, saying the same thing has happened to her computer. When you take the computer back to the shop, the assistant says that your computer has a **virus** that changed the look of your screen and sent itself to all the people in your e-mail address book.

The assistant then puts a program into your computer that is designed to stop other people from interfering with your computer.

>>
Computer problems such as viruses are frustrating.

The Internet and safety

A connection to the Internet is two-way. It allows you to easily share information. However, the story on the previous page shows how easy it is for somebody to get information from your computer or even control it without you knowing. People can also secretly put programs onto your computer. These programs could track what you are doing or they could damage other information on your computer.

What are the issues about Internet safety?

Millions of people are connected to the Internet because it is a very convenient way to send messages, find information, and run a business. The Internet makes it possible for large amounts of information to be copied and used with or without your permission. The problem is that people can be doing things with your computer without you even knowing about it. They could also be making your computer do things to other people's computers.

Q Do you think your computer should be completely safe?

Q Do you think there should be laws protecting your information?

Q Should governments control the Internet?

∨ Can we use the Internet without risking the safety of our information?

Who knows about you?

The Internet makes it very easy to store and share information about people. It can also be used to combine information in many ways, some that are useful and some that are not.

Governments, organizations, and large companies store a lot of information about a lot of people. Often this is stored on computer networks, which makes it easy to send to other people. The information may be your address, the size of your family, the cars you drive, where you shop, or whether you have been in trouble with the police.

Imagine that you pay for some film and film processing with your credit card over the Internet. The film shop would then have your banking details on their computer. They would also know how often you buy and use film. They could give these details to a company that sells cameras, who could send letters to you to try to persuade you to buy a digital camera.

Many countries are now introducing privacy laws to stop organizations and companies from sharing your information with others. The laws also insist that your information is stored safely.

▲ Computers can store a lot of information about how we live and work.

Quick byte

"Net nannies" are programs that parents and schools can use to stop young children from looking at unsuitable Web sites.

How safe is the Internet?

A connection to the Internet allows information to go to and from your computer. If you use the Internet to buy something, you may deliberately leave information about yourself, such as your address or bank account number. Some people use the Internet to steal your personal information.

∨∨ The information you send via the Internet travels through cables or is carried by radio waves.

Cookies

Information can be taken from your computer without your knowledge. When you visit a Web site, it might send you a **cookie**. A cookie is information that gets stored in your computer. Web sites can use cookies to record the number of times you visit the site. They can keep track of the pages you look at on the site. This can help the Web site owners to improve their Web site.

Hackers

Hackers are people who break into networks. Some hackers do not obey the law. They break into networks because they want to steal information or damage the network. If a hacker breaks into a bank network, they could steal credit card numbers to make purchases on the Internet.

Programs that change programs

If you are connected to the Internet, you can be sent programs that can change or destroy the information in your computer. Examples of these programs are viruses, **worms**, and **Trojan horses**. It is not always easy to tell the differences between these programs.

Viruses

Viruses attach copies of themselves to other programs. While a program is running, a virus can perform some other action, either harmless or harmful. Generally, viruses stay in one computer unless the computer user sends it to another computer.

However, a virus in an e-mail program could use the program to send itself to everyone listed in a personal address book and overload a network, slowing it down or stopping it.

Worms

Worms are programs that copy themselves to other machines using a network. The worms can then carry out harmless or harmful acts affecting millions of computers. If the worm copies itself many times on one computer, the computer has to slow down or even stop. In 2001, a hacker released a worm into the Internet. It copied itself over a quarter of a million times in half a day. This caused large sections of the Internet to slow down.

Trojan horses

Trojan horses are programs that are not what they appear to be. You might download a game from a Web site. When you begin to play the "game," the program destroys all the files in your computer. It gets its name from an ancient story about a large wooden horse, which was not what it appeared to be. It was presented as a gift but had enemy soldiers inside it.

▲ This computer program is looking for unwanted programs such as viruses.

Protecting information

One way of protecting information is to keep it on a floppy disk or a CD, and only use them on a computer that is not connected to the Internet. If a computer is connected to the Internet, some ways to protect computers include passwords and virus checkers.

Passwords

A password stops anyone else from using your computer (as long as they do not find out your password). It stops other people from accessing your files through the Internet. You can even use a password to allow only certain people to see your documents.

Quick byte

In the same way a locksmith can open your door if you have lost the key, special companies can help you if you forget your computer password.

Virus checkers

You can protect your computer from worms and viruses by putting special computer programs such as virus checkers onto your computer. Virus checkers find and destroy the virus before it does too much damage. Do not take programs from the Internet unless you are sure that they come from a safe source. If you are not certain about a computer program, buy it on a CD instead because it is less likely that a CD contains a virus.

^ The password on a computer is like the personal identification number (PIN) for a credit card.

>> Passwords are a common way of protecting computer information.

Network protection

Governments, businesses, and other organizations use enormous amounts of information. Computers in networks store this information so it can be obtained very quickly. These networks need to be protected—just imagine what may happen if businesses such as banks could not protect their computer networks!

Encryption

Encryption is the name given to the process of coding information so that only the person (or computer) with the right "decoding key" can unlock the code. This prevents people from reading information or taking information from a company's computer.

A company might put a coding program on all the computers in its network so that every time a document or message is created on the company's computers it is coded. Any other computer in the company can decode the message but computers outside the company's network cannot.

Firewalls

People who run networks may use a computer program called a **firewall**. Firewalls control what enters and leaves the network. They can also control who uses the network.

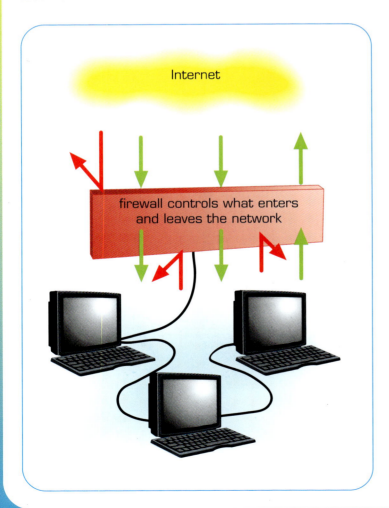

<<
A firewall is the name of one computer program that can protect a network. Some information is allowed through and some is not.

 # The Internet safety debate

The Internet is a very useful tool for sharing information all over the world. However, it allows people to find and misuse information. Do we always want to share all our information? What about our private information?

Arguments for

Some people feel the Internet is the best way to handle information because:

- ✓ businesses and industry need information from their customers in order to serve them better
- ✓ the more information is available, the easier it is to do research for projects
- ✓ governments need as much information as possible in order to plan their policies
- ✓ only those who have something to hide are worried about privacy.

Arguments against

Other people believe that the Internet should be carefully controlled because:

- ✗ business and industry might use the information to persuade us to buy things we do not need
- ✗ hackers can steal our information and programs such as viruses can damage it
- ✗ young children may find information that is unsuitable for them
- ✗ it is an invasion of personal privacy.

What is your opinion?

Q Should our privacy be protected?

Q Should people be able to use the Internet without any controls?

Q How can we control information people have about us?

Q Should other people be able to use our personal information without permission? What sorts of information should they be allowed to use?

« When you use the Internet, you leave a record behind.

 # Information ownership

The band

Some students set up a band at school. They decided to use the school computers to produce a music CD. First, to do their other school work, they downloaded information from the Internet. To give them extra time to make their CD, they only made a small number of changes to the Internet information they used for their school projects. They did not mention to their teacher which Web sites they had used.

The band worked very hard making their CD. They took their CDs to a shop, and the owner paid them a commission for each CD that was sold. Things went well for a while, then no one wanted to buy the CD, even though the music was very popular.

One day they discovered why. The CD was being sold very cheaply at a local market. Someone had made copies of the CD without getting permission from the band or the shop. They had broken the band's **copyright** on its music.

Does the band have a right to complain to the shop when they had pretended that other people's work was their own in their school projects?

<< The music on CDs is owned by the creator of the music. You cannot copy it without permission.

Copyright

Copyright is a legal right of someone to control what happens to any work they have created, such as music played by a band. Creators such as authors, photographers, and artists automatically have copyright of their works unless they agree to give it to someone else.

If a person owns the copyright on a piece of work, no one else can legally use it without permission from the copyright owner. Usually you have to pay the owner of the copyright to use their work. The copyright symbol © appears on the second page of this book.

>>
This image is copyright. The book publishers had to pay a fee to use it.

What are the issues about copyright?

Computers have made it very easy to copy information. People can use special equipment to copy other people's photos and art. Words, pictures, and music can be downloaded from the Internet. Copyright laws are different in different countries, so it is difficult to decide which country's laws apply to the Internet because it can be used all over the world.

Should people copy without asking permission?

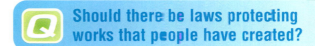
Should there be laws protecting works that people have created?

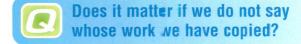
Does it matter if we do not say whose work we have copied?

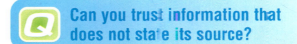
Can you trust information that does not state its source?

Protecting images

Computers and the Internet have made it easy to copy pictures, such as photographs, computer graphics, and paintings, and send them all over the world.

A scanner copies pictures into a computer. Special computer programs allow you to alter a picture by changing the colors, brightness, or shapes of the different parts of the picture. A person can have their eyebrows made bushier or their nose shorter.

>>
Scanners can be used to copy text and pictures into computers.

Watermarks

There are ways to protect the rights of copyright owners. You can use a computer to put a complex mark on a picture on the computer screen. Every time someone looks at the picture they will see this mark. The mark is difficult to remove so that someone who wants to copy a picture without permission will have to spend a long time getting rid of the mark. The mark makes the picture hard to view, so an invisible mark can also be put into the picture. The invisible mark is actually a program, which stops your computer from copying the picture.

Watermarks can be used by people to check where a picture has come from or whether it is a fake.

Downloading music

Some Internet downloads are legal and some are illegal. A download is legal if permission is obtained from the copyright owner, who may also get a payment. Downloading is illegal if copyright rules are not followed.

Downloading legally

Some companies use the Internet to sell music. They will only send you the music if you give them your credit card details. These companies act legally if they pay money to the copyright owner of the music every time they make a sale.

Some computer programs let you copy music. These programs can be used legally to download music if the copyright owner has agreed to make their music freely available on the Internet.

Downloading illegally

Some computer programs can be used to make illegal copies of music. It is illegal to copy music if the copyright owner has not agreed to make the music freely available on the Internet. This means the copyright owner is not acknowledged and they do not receive any payment for that copy of the music.

>> Musicians spend a lot of time and money recording an album. Copyright fees supply their incomes and pay some of their expenses.

Some companies act illegally by selling a list, which tells people where they can get the music they want. Most of this music is supplied without permission. These companies say they are just delivering music, just as the mail delivers letters. They say they cannot be accused of copying music without permission or payment. However, the creators of the music do not receive any payment.

Is information reliable?

When people use the Internet to find information, they want to know that it is coming from a source that can be trusted. If the source or the creator of the information has been acknowledged, then it is much easier to check the accuracy of the information.

Checking information

Many Web sites are created by governments, big companies, or universities. These Web sites are usually trustworthy because of the good name of the organization that created the Web site. A trustworthy Web site will contain details of how you can contact the organization that runs it. Other Web sites are run by individual people or small organizations. It is hard to know whether to trust the information these Web sites contain because they may not have been checked. If you are looking for information on the Internet for a school project, it is always a good idea to check three different Web sites. If they all give you the same information, then it is more likely to be correct.

Triple-check your information when you are doing Internet research.

Quick byte

When you are preparing a school report or project you need to make a list of the sources of information you use. You should do this for Web sites as well as for books.

Checking the user

The owners of a Web site might want the Web site users to prove their identities. A bank might check the people wanting to use their Web site. They will only allow people to use their Web site if a correct password is entered. A padlock or key symbol is often used to show a Web site is secure.

 # The information ownership debate

A huge amount of information is available on the Internet. Some of the information is freely available. Other information can only be copied after obtaining special permission from the copyright holder. Sometimes it is difficult to know what to do because different countries have different laws about Internet copyright.

Arguments for

Some people believe that copyright laws on the Internet are important because:

- ✓ the copyright owner is acknowledged and paid for their work
- ✓ sources identifying the copyright owner can be easily checked for accuracy
- ✓ credit is given to the creator and not someone else who may copy the work
- ✓ reminding people about copyright may stop them from copying.

Arguments against

Other people believe that Internet copyright is a problem because:

- ✗ some people are prevented from obtaining information because they cannot afford to pay for it
- ✗ everyone will benefit from the Internet if there are no copyright laws
- ✗ the rules are hard to follow because copyright laws are different in different countries.

What is your opinion?

- **Q** How can one country apply its laws to the Internet when the Internet can be used anywhere in the world?
- **Q** Does copyright actually prevent people copying from the Internet without permission?
- **Q** Do we need new copyright laws for the Internet?

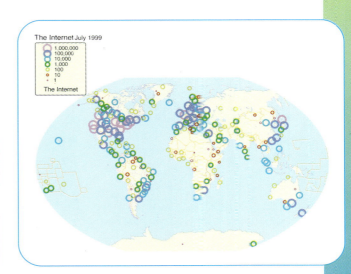

^ The Internet may be worldwide but not everyone can afford to use it.

Electronic storage of information

Old information

A student tells her teacher that her mother has just thrown away some old computer disks. Her mother had tried to use them on her computer, but she discovered that the computer wasn't working. When she took the computer for repair, she was told that it was too out of date and there were no spare parts. Even worse, the assistant had told her that no modern computer could get the information off the old disks. All the information was lost!

The teacher decides to take her students to a museum to look at the ways people kept information in the past.

The students see pens, pencils, typewriters, and printing presses. They see writing on stone tablets, very old books, and paper scrolls. This writing can still be read even though some of it was written over 3,000 years ago.

On the bus going home, the students and their teacher discuss how long they think information in their computers and disks will last.

>>
The writing on this stone is over 2,000 years old. We do not need a computer to read it. Will anyone be able to read our computer disks in 2,000 years' time?

Storing information

Before computers, people kept nearly all of their information on paper. Business documents, government records, school reports, diaries, and bank account details were mainly stored on paper.

A lot of information is now stored electronically on computers. New computers, computer programs, and ways of storing information are being developed all the time.

What are the issues about electronic storage?

New computers can store and process large quantities of information. However, they are not always able to obtain the information stored on older disks. If people want to read these disks they often have to keep their previous computers. These are difficult to repair if spare parts are no longer available. If we cannot obtain the information on our old disks and computers, then it may be lost forever.

Why do we use computers to store information?

How long will electronic information last?

Should new computers be designed to use old as well as new disks?

▼ The disks that are used to store computer files keep changing.

Why store information in computers?

Using computers to store information has advantages. It saves space and paper. Computers store huge amounts of information in a very small space. Computer disks are much easier to carry around than books. Electronic information can be updated very quickly.

Many experts predicted that computers would make the "paperless office." Important letters and records would be stored in computers instead of on paper. In fact, offices are using much more paper since computers were invented. Everyone prints out their information on paper as well as storing it on computer!

Information stored on computers can be found quickly and easily. Many computer programs use key words to search through information. A computer can be used to quickly find all the files containing a certain word. If the information was stored on paper, you would have to read every file until you found the key word, which might take days or weeks!

It is much easier to correct your mistakes on a computer than on a handwritten page. It is also much quicker and easier to use the Internet to send your writing to someone else.

^ This person is using a computer called a palmtop. Computer storage uses up very little space but contains huge amounts of information.

Quick byte

A floppy disk can store about three books, each with 300 pages with 200 words on a page. A CD can store more than 300 times as much.

Safe storage and handling

Computer information can be stored either outside or inside the computer. Floppy disks, CDs, and digital video/versatile disks (DVDs) store information outside the computer. Hard drives can be used for storing information both inside and outside the computer. Microchips are also used to store information inside the computer.

Magnetic storage

Disks and hard drives use a special magnetic material to store information. The information on disks can be lost if the disk is damaged. If the disk comes into contact with other magnetic material, such as credit card strips, the information that is stored on them can be altered or destroyed.

CDs and DVDs

CDs and DVDs are not made of magnetic material and so they are not damaged by magnets. However, they can be easily damaged if they are handled badly. Care must be taken not to scratch the disk.

> **Quick byte**
> A new computer chip, called a millipede chip, which is the size of a postage stamp, is being developed. It can store 10 to 15 times more than a normal chip. This is the same amount of information that can be stored on 200 CDs.

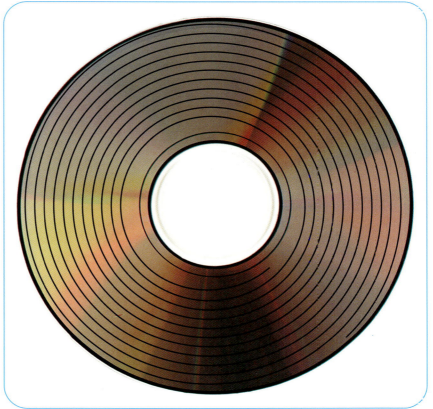

>>
The information on a CD is stored on a track that is 3 miles (almost 5 km) long! This is how so much information can be stored on it even though it is very thin.

How long will electronic information last?

If electronic information is looked after carefully, it will last a long time. However, just as paper or cloth can fade and wood can rot, computer disks can wear out because of the conditions around them. Information can only be kept if it is copied onto fresh disks before the old ones wear out.

If information is stored on old disks, the computer that was used to create the information is needed to read the information. If the information is valuable, the computer may need to be repaired or built again. However, as the years go by, this becomes difficult because technicians are no longer trained to fix the old models and the plans may be lost.

Quick byte
The first floppy disks were 8 inches (20 cm) across and could be bent easily. That is why they were called "floppy."

<<
It is difficult to find people to repair old computers.

There is a bigger problem. Every year computer companies produce new computers and different versions of computer programs. The companies want us to buy the new computers and programs because they are better than the previous ones. The new computers cannot always use the information stored on the old disks. When this happens, the old machines and programs become useless.

 # The electronic storage debate

Computers and the Internet have made it very easy to produce and store huge amounts of information. Do we need to keep this information? If so, how do we store it so it can be read by future generations? If not, how do we decide what to get rid of?

Arguments against

Other people feel that paper information is best and only small amounts of electronic information need to be kept because:

- ✗ the disks that you store the information on will not work in the future
- ✗ it will be too expensive to keep all the old computers working
- ✗ much of the information is not important
- ✗ a lot of information from the past has already been lost.

Arguments for

Some people believe that electronic storage is the best way to keep information because:

- ✓ a lot of information can be kept in a small space
- ✓ it saves paper
- ✓ people can find information quickly and easily for research
- ✓ changing, correcting, updating, and sending information is easier.

What is your opinion?

 **Q** Should we stop making better and better computers if we cannot use the information produced by older computers?

 **Q** Should we think more carefully about storing information on paper as well as on computers and disks?

▽ Should we save all of our information?

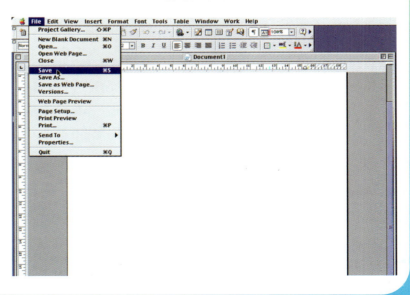

Summary

Computers allow people to get information easily and quickly from all over the world. People are able to take many different types of information and mix them together to create new forms of information. Computers and the Internet have changed the way we look at many issues such as privacy, copyright, and preservation of information. In this book, some of the issues that surround information technology have been raised.

ISSUE 1 — Internet safety

- The Internet is a useful tool for sharing information.
- The Internet makes it possible for people to access information from your computer without your permission.
- There are many ways to prevent people from misusing the Internet.

Q: Should you know who is storing information about you?

ISSUE 2 — Information ownership

- Computers and the Internet have made it easy to use other people's information.
- The Internet has made it easier to ignore copyright laws.
- Different countries have different laws about Internet copyright.

Q: How can one country apply its laws to the Internet when the Internet is everywhere?

ISSUE 3 — Electronic storage of information

- Computers can store enormous amounts of information in a small space.
- Computers are continually being improved—they are becoming smaller, faster, and more versatile.
- Many new computers cannot use the information stored on disks used by older computers.

Q: Should computer companies worry about preserving information if their job is to make better computers?

THE FUTURE

By 2050, computers may be the size of a watch face because manufacturers are constantly seeking new ways of designing faster and smaller computers.

Glossary

browser	a computer program that displays Web pages
computer programs	sets of instructions telling the computer what to do
cookie	information put in your computer by a server to track what you did when you looked at a Web site on that server
copyright	the legal right of someone to control the work they have created
downloads	takes information, such as music, from the Internet
e-mail	electronic mail, which passes as an electronic message from one computer to another through a network
encryption	a way of coding information so that only certain people or computers can change it into understandable language
firewall	a computer program used to protect a network
hackers	people who break into networks
information technology	the ways that computers can be used to process information
input device	a device that takes information into the computer; for example, a mouse
Internet	millions of computer networks connected together across the planet
memory	the place in which information and programs are stored while the computer is working
network computers	computers that send messages from one network to another
networks	collections of computers connected together; for example, in a school or business
output device	a device that sends information out from the computer; for example, printers and speakers
processor	the part of a computer that changes inputs to outputs and controls the output devices
server	a computer found inside a network. It provides a service to the computers connected to it.
Trojan horses	disguised computer programs that destroy the files in your computer
virus	a computer program that attaches copies of itself to another program
Web	short for World Wide Web, a worldwide collection of millions of linked computer files
Web pages	electronic "pages" stored on a server. Other computers use browsers to find them.
Web sites	collections of related Web pages; for example, a school Web site
worms	computer programs that can copy themselves many times and possibly cause damage to computers in a network

Index

B
binary code 8
browser 9

C
CDs 7, 15, 18, 27
computer programs 4, 7, 10, 14, 15, 16, 21, 25
cookies 13
copyright 18, 19, 21, 23, 30

D
downloading 4, 18, 19, 21
DVDs 27

E
e-mail 10, 14
encryption 16

F
firewalls 16
floppy disks 26, 27, 28

H
hackers 13, 14, 17

I
information ownership 4, 5, 18–23, 30
information storage 4, 5, 24–29, 30
input devices 6, 7
Internet 4, 5, 9–17, 18, 19, 20, 21, 22, 26, 29, 30

M
magnetic storage 27
memory 6
music 18, 19, 21

N
networks 9, 13, 14, 16
network computers 9, 16

O
output devices 6, 7

P
paper 25, 26, 29
passwords 15
privacy 5, 11, 12, 17, 30
processor 6

S
scanner 20
server 9
switches 8

T
Trojan horses 14

V
viruses 10, 14, 15
virus checkers 15

W
watermarks 20
Web pages 9
Web sites 9, 10, 22
worms 14, 15

9796 457 928